ADHD MASTERY FOR PARENTS

How to Raise ADHD Kids without Stress and Negative Emotions. A Simple Step-by-Step Guide for Parents.

Dr. Maya Martin

Copyright © 2024 by Dr. Maya Martin

CONTENTS

DEDICATION

To the Reader

In the quiet moments between the turning of these pages, to you, dear reader, this work is affectionately dedicated. You are the voyager in this literary journey, navigating the words and worlds within. Your imagination breathes life into the tales woven here, and your curiosity is the compass guiding the narrative.

May these words serve as companions on your literary adventures, offering solace, inspiration, and perhaps a touch of magic. It is your presence that transforms mere text into a shared experience, and for that, I am truly grateful.

With sincere appreciation,

Dr. Maya Martin

Introduction

Welcome to " ADHD Mastery for Parents"!

Parenting is a journey filled with joys, challenges, and an abundance of learning. When your child has Attention Deficit Hyperactivity Disorder (ADHD), the journey can become even more intricate. This book is designed as a guide and companion for parents navigating the unique landscape of raising children with ADHD.

Understanding the Path Ahead

In this comprehensive guide, we delve into the intricacies of ADHD, exploring its nuances, diagnosis, and treatment options. As parents, it's crucial to have a solid understanding of what ADHD entails to provide the best support for our children.

Practical Strategies for Everyday Challenges

Parenting a tween with ADHD comes with its own set of hurdles. From understanding your child's "Executive Age" to mastering effective reward systems and collaborating with teachers, we'll explore practical strategies to navigate these challenges.

Holistic Approach to Development

Beyond behavioral aspects, this book delves into cultivating healthy habits, enhancing social skills, managing emotions, and structuring daily routines. Each chapter provides actionable insights to foster your child's overall development, from physical well-being to emotional resilience.

Empowering Parents for Success

Remember, as a parent, your well-being is just as important. The final chapters focus on self-care, reminding you that taking care of yourself allows you to be the best advocate and support for your child.

Let this book be your companion on this unique parenting journey. Together, let's embrace the challenges, celebrate the victories, and create a nurturing environment where your child can thrive.

Here's to empowering you and your child on this remarkable adventure!

Chapter 1: Understanding ADHD

What Is ADHD?

Attention Deficit Hyperactivity Disorder (ADHD) is more than just a diagnosis; it's a unique way of experiencing the world. In this chapter, we embark on a journey to unravel the complexities of ADHD, gaining insights that will empower you as a parent.

Unveiling ADHD: Beyond the Surface

ADHD is not a one-size-fits-all condition. We explore the diverse manifestations and variations of ADHD, understanding that each child's experience is distinctive. From inattentiveness to hyperactivity and impulsivity, we dissect the core components that define ADHD.

Navigating the Diagnostic Landscape

How is ADHD diagnosed? Understanding the diagnostic process is crucial for parents seeking clarity. We delve into the assessments, evaluations, and criteria that professionals use to identify ADHD, empowering you to actively engage in the diagnostic journey.

A Glimpse into the ADHD Brain

To comprehend ADHD is to understand the intricacies of the brain. We explore the neurological aspects that underlie ADHD, shedding light on how differences in brain structure and function contribute to the challenges and strengths associated with the condition.

Dispelling Myths and Embracing Realities

ADHD is often surrounded by misconceptions. We debunk common myths, providing a foundation for informed and compassionate parenting. By separating fact from fiction, you'll be better equipped to support your child on their unique path.

The Individual Journey

As we navigate this chapter, remember that ADHD is a spectrum, and each child's journey is distinctive. By gaining a deeper understanding of what ADHD truly is, you lay the groundwork for a more empathetic and effective approach to parenting.

Let's embark on this exploration together, fostering a foundation of knowledge that will empower you on your parenting journey with

an ADHD child.

Chapter 2: Navigating Treatment Options

Diagnosing ADHD

Before we embark on the journey of understanding and implementing effective treatments, we must first navigate the terrain of diagnosis. In this chapter, we unravel the intricacies of diagnosing Attention Deficit Hyperactivity Disorder (ADHD) and set the stage for informed decision-making.

The Diagnostic Process

Understanding how ADHD is diagnosed is crucial for parents seeking answers. We walk through the diagnostic process, from initial concerns to assessments conducted by healthcare professionals. By demystifying the steps involved, you gain insight into the journey towards clarity.

Signs and Symptoms

What are the telltale signs of ADHD? Recognizing the behavioral and cognitive patterns associated with ADHD is a fundamental aspect of the diagnostic journey. We delve into the various manifestations, providing a comprehensive overview to aid parents in identifying potential symptoms in their children.

Collaborative Diagnosis

Diagnosing ADHD is not a solitary endeavor. Parents play a vital role in the diagnostic process. We explore how collaborative efforts between parents, educators, and healthcare professionals contribute to a more accurate and holistic understanding of a child's needs.

Approaches to ADHD Treatment

With a diagnosis in hand, the next step is navigating the diverse landscape of treatment options. In this section, we explore various approaches to managing ADHD, recognizing that each child's journey is unique.

Multidimensional Treatment Strategies

ADHD treatment is not one-size-fits-all. We delve into the multidimensional strategies that encompass behavioral interventions, educational support, and, in some cases, medication. Understanding the range of options empowers parents to make informed decisions aligned with their child's individual needs.

Lifestyle Modifications

Beyond formal interventions, we explore the impact of lifestyle modifications on ADHD management. From dietary considerations to sleep patterns, we uncover how simple yet significant changes can positively influence a child's well-being.

Collaborating with Professionals

Building a support network is essential in navigating ADHD treatment. We discuss the importance of collaboration with healthcare providers, therapists, and educators, emphasizing the role of teamwork in ensuring the best outcomes for your child.

Holistic Wellness

Treatment goes beyond symptom management; it extends to fostering holistic well-being. We explore how a comprehensive approach, addressing both physical and emotional aspects, contributes to the overall success and happiness of children with ADHD.

As we navigate the diverse landscape of ADHD diagnosis and treatment, remember that knowledge is a powerful tool. By understanding the options available, you empower yourself to make informed decisions that resonate with the unique needs of your child.

Chapter 3: Effective Parenting Strategies for Tweens with ADHD

Parenting a tween with ADHD requires a unique set of strategies and approaches. In this chapter, we explore practical and effective ways to navigate the challenges and celebrate the strengths of your child during this transitional phase.

Assessing Your Child's "Executive Age"

Understanding your tween's cognitive development is key to tailoring your parenting approach. We delve into the concept of "Executive Age," exploring the cognitive functions that influence decision-making, planning, and organization. By assessing your child's executive functions, you gain valuable insights to adapt your parenting style to their evolving needs.

Mastering the "Reward System"

One of the cornerstones of effective parenting for ADHD tweens is mastering the art of the reward system. We explore how positive reinforcement can be a powerful tool in shaping behavior and fostering motivation. Learn practical strategies to implement a reward system that resonates with your child, promoting positive habits and accomplishments.

Collaborating with Teachers

Building a strong partnership with your child's educators is essential for a supportive academic environment. We discuss effective communication strategies, sharing insights with teachers, and collaborating on tailored approaches to enhance your child's learning experience. A collaborative effort between home and school is crucial for your tween's success.

Dos and Don'ts for Effective Parenting

Parenting is a journey of trial and error, and it becomes even more nuanced when ADHD is part of the equation. We provide a practical guide of dos and don'ts, drawing on real-life experiences and expert advice. From setting realistic expectations to fostering open communication, these guidelines aim to empower you as a parent navigating the unique challenges of raising a tween with ADHD.

Nurturing Individuality

Throughout this chapter, we emphasize the importance of recognizing and celebrating your tween's individual strengths and talents. By embracing their uniqueness, you create a supportive environment that encourages self-confidence and resilience.

Parenting tweens with ADHD requires patience, adaptability, and a deep understanding of your child's evolving needs. As we explore these effective strategies, remember that you are not alone on this journey. Together, let's navigate the path to fostering a positive and nurturing environment for your tween with ADHD.

Chapter 4: Cultivating Healthy Habits

Promoting Physical Activity and Outdoor Time

Physical activity plays a crucial role in the well-being of children with ADHD. In this section, we explore the benefits of promoting regular physical activity and outdoor time. From structured activities to unstructured play, discover how movement can positively impact your child's focus, mood, and overall health.

Teaching Proper Nutrition

Nutrition is the fuel that powers both body and mind. We delve into the importance of a balanced and nutritious diet for children with

ADHD. Learn about foods that support cognitive function, strategies for managing dietary challenges, and how making mindful nutritional choices can contribute to your child's overall well-being.

Establishing Good Sleep Patterns

Quality sleep is foundational for every child's development, but it holds particular significance for those with ADHD. In this section, we explore the relationship between sleep and ADHD symptoms. Discover practical tips for establishing good sleep patterns, creating a bedtime routine, and addressing common sleep challenges faced by children with ADHD.

Successful Potty Training

Navigating potty training can be a unique journey for parents of children with ADHD. We discuss effective strategies and considerations for successful potty training tailored to the specific needs of your child. From patience to consistency, learn how to make this developmental milestone a positive and achievable experience.

Maintaining Personal Hygiene

Personal hygiene is an essential aspect of daily life, and it becomes a valuable skill for children with ADHD to master. We explore practical tips for teaching and maintaining good personal hygiene habits. From establishing routines to making hygiene activities enjoyable, discover strategies to instill these habits in a positive and supportive manner.

Throughout this chapter, we emphasize the holistic approach to cultivating healthy habits. Each section provides actionable insights to help you integrate these habits seamlessly into your child's daily routine. By fostering a healthy lifestyle, you contribute to their overall well-being and set the foundation for a positive and thriving future.

Chapter 5: Enhancing Social Skills

Understanding ADHD's Impact on Social Competence

Social interactions are a vital aspect of a child's development, yet for those with ADHD, navigating social situations can be uniquely challenging. In this section, we delve into how ADHD influences social competence, exploring the nuances that shape your child's interactions with peers and the world around them.

Developing Social Executive Function Skills

Social skills are the building blocks of meaningful connections. We explore the role of executive functions in shaping social behaviors. From understanding social cues to effective communication, discover strategies to develop and enhance the social executive function skills crucial for successful interactions.

Fostering Friendship

Building and maintaining friendships is a significant aspect of a child's social development. We discuss practical approaches to foster meaningful friendships for children with ADHD. From facilitating social opportunities to teaching effective communication, learn how to create a supportive environment for lasting connections.

Behavior Improvement Strategies

Positive social interactions often hinge on behavior. In this section, we explore behavior improvement strategies tailored to enhance your child's social skills. From reinforcing positive behaviors to addressing challenges, discover effective approaches that contribute to your child's success in social settings.

Addressing Bullying

Children with ADHD may be more susceptible to bullying, making it crucial to address this issue proactively. We discuss signs of bullying, strategies to empower your child, and effective communication with educators. By fostering resilience and providing support, you can help your child navigate and overcome challenges related to bullying.

Throughout this chapter, the focus is on empowering your child with ADHD to navigate the complexities of social interactions successfully. By understanding the impact of ADHD on social competence and implementing targeted strategies, you play a pivotal role in fostering your child's social growth and helping them build fulfilling connections with others.

Chapter 6: Emotional Well-being

Coping with Emotional Hypersensitivity

Emotions are a powerful force in every child's life, and for those with ADHD, emotional hypersensitivity can be an added challenge. In this section, we explore the intricacies of emotional hypersensitivity, offering insights into how it manifests in children with ADHD and providing practical coping strategies for both parents and children.

Importance of Emotional Regulation

Emotional regulation is a fundamental skill that influences a child's ability to navigate daily challenges. We delve into the significance of emotional regulation for children with ADHD, offering practical guidance on fostering this crucial skill. Learn strategies to help your child recognize, understand, and manage their emotions in a healthy and constructive manner.

Anger Management Techniques for ADHD Kids

Anger is a natural emotion, but managing it can be particularly challenging for children with ADHD. In this section, we explore effective anger management techniques tailored to the unique needs of ADHD kids. From mindfulness practices to communication strategies, discover tools to help your child express and manage anger in a constructive way.

Throughout this chapter, the focus is on nurturing your child's emotional well-being. By understanding and addressing emotional hypersensitivity, promoting emotional regulation, and providing effective anger management techniques, you contribute to your child's overall mental health and resilience. Embracing and guiding their emotional journey empowers them to face life's challenges with confidence and self-awareness.

Chapter 7: Structured Living for Calmness

Constructing a Daily Routine

Structure and routine provide a sense of stability that can be particularly beneficial for children with ADHD. In this section, we explore the importance of constructing a daily routine and how it serves as a foundation for creating a calm and predictable environment. Discover the elements that contribute to an effective routine and how consistency can positively impact your child's daily life.

Tips for Establishing Your Child's Routine or Schedule

Establishing a routine tailored to your child's unique needs is an art that requires careful consideration. We provide practical tips for creating a schedule that aligns with your child's strengths and challenges. From incorporating flexibility to involving your child in the planning process, learn how to craft a routine that promotes a sense of order and security.

The Power of Predictability

Children with ADHD often thrive in environments where they know what to expect. We discuss the power of predictability and how a well-constructed routine can reduce anxiety, improve focus, and create a more harmonious living space.

Balancing Structure and Flexibility

While structure is essential, flexibility is equally important. We explore the delicate balance between having a structured routine and allowing room for spontaneity. Discover how to adapt the routine to accommodate unexpected changes while maintaining a sense of order.

Involving Your Child in the Process

Empower your child by involving them in the creation of their routine. We share strategies for collaborative planning, allowing your child to have a voice in their daily schedule. This not only fosters a sense of responsibility but also enhances their engagement with the routine.

No routine is perfect, and challenges may arise. We provide guidance on identifying potential obstacles and making necessary adjustments to the routine. Flexibility and adaptability are key as you work to create a structured living environment that suits your child's evolving needs.

By implementing a well-thought-out routine, you provide a framework that promotes calmness, enhances focus, and instills a sense of security for your child with ADHD. This chapter aims to guide you in constructing a structured living space that contributes to a positive and thriving daily experience.

Chapter 8: Equipping for Life Success

Defining Life Skills

Life skills are the building blocks that empower individuals to navigate the complexities of daily life successfully. In this section, we explore the concept of life skills and identify the essential abilities that contribute to a child's overall development. From communication to problem-solving, discover the fundamental skills that pave the way for lifelong success.

Understanding Their Importance

Life skills go beyond academic achievements, playing a crucial role in shaping a child's character and future. We delve into the importance of instilling life skills in children with ADHD, emphasizing how these skills contribute to resilience, adaptability, and a sense of competency. Learn how fostering life skills sets the stage for independence and success in various aspects of life.

Introducing Chores

Chores are more than just tasks; they are opportunities for learning and growth. In this section, we discuss the significance of introducing chores to children with ADHD. From building a sense of responsibility to developing practical life skills, discover the positive impact chores can have on your child's development.

Chores as Learning Opportunities

Chores provide a hands-on approach to learning valuable life skills. We explore how tasks such as organizing, cleaning, and time management during chores contribute to the development of essential skills that extend far beyond the completion of the task itself.

Fostering Independence

Empowering your child with ADHD to take on age-appropriate responsibilities fosters a sense of independence. We discuss how introducing chores can boost self-esteem, improve decision-making, and instill a sense of pride in their capabilities.

Tailoring Chores to Individual Abilities

Every child is unique, and so are their strengths and challenges. We provide guidance on tailoring chores to align with your child's abilities, ensuring that the tasks assigned are both meaningful and achievable. This approach creates a positive and supportive environment for skill development.

Celebrating Achievements

Acknowledging and celebrating your child's efforts in completing chores is vital for reinforcing positive behaviors. We discuss the importance of positive reinforcement, offering praise, and creating a sense of accomplishment that motivates continued engagement in life skills development.

By understanding and embracing the significance of life skills, particularly through the introduction of chores, you equip your child with ADHD for success in various aspects of life. This chapter aims to guide you in fostering a foundation of skills that will empower your child to navigate the journey ahead with confidence and competence.

Chapter 9: Parental Self-Care

What Is Self-Care?

Parenting is a demanding journey, especially when navigating the unique challenges of raising a child with ADHD. In this section, we explore the concept of self-care and why it's not just a luxury but a necessity for parents. Understanding the importance of self-care lays the foundation for building resilience and maintaining a positive and healthy parenting experience.

Redefining Self-Care

Self-care goes beyond indulgence; it's a holistic approach to nurturing your physical, emotional, and mental well-being. We delve into the various dimensions of self-care, emphasizing its role in fostering a balanced and sustainable lifestyle for parents.

Recognizing Burnout

Parental burnout is a real concern, and it's essential to recognize the signs. We discuss the impact of chronic stress on parents and how self-care acts as a protective measure against burnout. By understanding your own needs, you can cultivate a healthier and more sustainable parenting approach.

Practical Self-Care Tips for Parents

With a clear understanding of the importance of self-care, we move into actionable strategies to integrate self-care into your daily routine. These practical tips are designed to be achievable, even in the midst of a busy schedule, providing you with the tools to prioritize your well-being.

Carving Out Time for Yourself

Time is a precious commodity for parents, but carving out moments for self-care is crucial. We explore realistic ways to allocate time for self-care, whether it's a few minutes of mindfulness or a longer break for rejuvenation.

Building a Support Network

Self-care extends beyond individual efforts; it involves creating a supportive network. We discuss the importance of seeking help, connecting with others who understand your journey, and building a community that fosters mutual support.

Embracing Imperfection

Parenting is a journey filled with highs and lows, and it's essential to embrace imperfection. We provide insights into letting go of perfectionism, accepting that it's okay not to have all the answers, and finding joy in the small victories.

Sustainable Self-Care Practices

The key to successful self-care is sustainability. We explore practices that can be consistently integrated into your routine, ensuring that self-care becomes an ongoing and integral part of your parenting journey.

By prioritizing self-care, you not only enhance your own well-being but also create a more nurturing and resilient environment for your child. This chapter aims to empower you with practical tools and insights to make self-care an essential aspect of your parenting routine.